First published 2000 by Walker Books Ltd
87 Vauxhall Walk, London SE11 5HJ
This edition produced 2000 for The Book People Ltd
Hall Wood Avenue, Haydock, St Helens WA11 9UL

Text © 2000 Walker Books Ltd
Illustrations © 1988, 1991, 1996, 1999 Barbara Firth
Cover illustration © 2000 Barbara Firth

2 4 6 8 10 9 7 5 3 1

This book has been typeset in Columbus.

Printed in Hong Kong

British Library Cataloguing in Publication Data.
A catalogue record for this book is available
from the British Library.

ISBN 0-7445-7518-4

LITTLE BEAR'S BABY BOOK

All about _____

Place picture here

This is the first picture of me ever.

Based on the **Big Bear and Little Bear** *stories*
Written by **Martin Waddell** *Illustrated by* **Barbara Firth**

We love you, Little Bear

My mum's name is _____ .

My dad's name is _____ .

Some other people in my family are _____

_____ .

Place picture here

Here is a photograph of my family.

Let's begin at the beginning, Little Bear

The date I was due to

be born was

_____ .

The doctor told

Mum to stop eating

certain things.

What she missed most

was _____

_____ .

Mum thought I would be a

girl   boy

Dad thought I would be a

girl   boy

Some of the names they thought about were

_____

_____ .

Mum and Dad first heard my heart beat on _____ .

The date they felt my first kick was _____ .

Here is a picture

of my scan at

_____ *weeks.*

Being born

The date I was born was _____ .

The place was _____ .

The time was _____ .

The colour of my eyes was _____ .

I weighed _____ .

I measured _____ .

This is how Mum and Dad
let everyone know I had arrived.

When you were tiny, Little Bear

My first home was at _____ .

Some of my first visitors were _____

_____ .

Some of my first presents were _____

_____

_____

_____

_____

_____ .

*Here is a lock
of my hair.*

Place picture here

*Here is a
photograph of
me when I was
one week old.*

Congratulations!

Mum and Dad received lots of cards.
Here are some of their favourites.

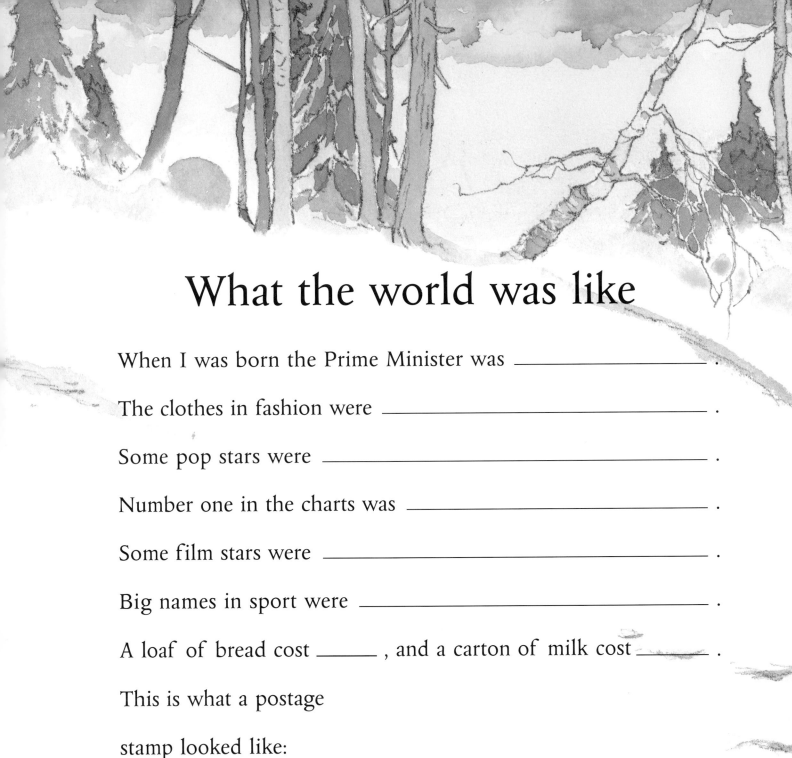

What the world was like

When I was born the Prime Minister was _____ .

The clothes in fashion were _____ .

Some pop stars were _____ .

Number one in the charts was _____ .

Some film stars were _____ .

Big names in sport were _____ .

A loaf of bread cost _____ , and a carton of milk cost _____ .

This is what a postage

stamp looked like:

Aren't you clever,
Little Bear!

I first slept through

the night when

I was _____ old.

I first held my head up

when I was _____ old.

I first rolled over when I was _____ old.

I first sat up alone when I was _____ old.

I first shuffled on my bottom when I was _____ old.

I first crawled when I was _____ old.

Hands

I first played with my hands when I

was _____ old.

I first reached for a toy when I

was _____ old.

I first clapped my hands when I

was _____ old.

I first waved bye-bye when I was _____ old.

Here is my hand print

aged _____ .

Feet

I first stood by myself when I was _____ old.

I took my first step when I was _____ old.

I went for my first walk outside

when I was _____

_____ old.

Here is my

foot print

aged _____ .

Eat up, Little Bear!

I first tasted solid food when I was _____ old.

It was _____

_____ .

I first sat in a highchair when I was _____ old.

I first drank from a cup when I was _____ old.

I first held a spoon when I was _____ old.

The foods I liked were _____

_____

_____ .

The foods I least liked were _____

_____

_____ .

Teething

I cut my first tooth when

I was _____ old.

The first thing I bit was

_____ .

I cut my second tooth when

I was _____ old.

I cut my third tooth when

I was _____ old.

I cut my fourth tooth when I

was _____ old.

Time for bed, Little Bear

I first slept in my cot when

I was _____ old.

Some of the things

I did before I went to bed

were _____

_____ .

My favourite bedtime toy was _____ .

My favourite lullabies were _____

_____

_____ .

My favourite bedtime story was

_____

_____ .

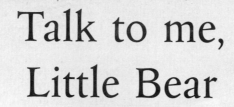

Talk to me,
Little Bear

I first smiled when I was _____ old.

I first laughed when I was _____ old.

I first copied noises when I was _____ old.

My very first word was _____ .

Other first words and sayings were _____

_____ .

My first name for Mum was _____ .

My first name for Dad was _____ .

My favourite nursery rhymes were _____

_____

_____ .

Let's play, Little Bear

Games I liked playing

were _____

_____ .

My first friends were _____

_____

_____ .

My favourite toy was _____ .

My favourite book was _____ .

Things that made me laugh were _____

_____ .

Place picture here

Here is a photograph of me and my friends.

The most ticklish

bit of me was

_____ .

Feeling poorly

My first illness was _____ .

This is what Mum and Dad did to help me get

better: _____

_____

_____

_____

_____ .

My doctor's name was _____ .

Some of the illnesses I was immunised against

were _____

_____

_____ .

First holiday

I went on my first holiday when I was _____ old.

We went to _____

_____

_____

These are some of the things we did: _____

_____

_____

_____

_____

_____

_____ .

What I liked best about the holiday was _____

_____

_____

_____

_____

_____

_____

_____

_____ .

Happy birthday,
Little Bear

This is how Mum and Dad celebrated my first birthday:

_____

_____

_____

_____

_____

_____ .

These are some of the presents I received:

_____

_____

_____ .

Here I am on my first birthday.

Place picture here

Second birthday

This is how we celebrated my second birthday: _____

_____

_____ .

These are the people who were there: _____

_____

_____ .

The games we played were _____

_____

_____ .

These are some of the presents I received: _____

_____

_____ .

Place picture here

Here I am on my second birthday.

Look how you've grown, Little Bear!

Date	Age	Height	Weight

Special memories

Special memories